90-Day Devotional Journal for Women

90-Day
Devotional
Journal
for Women

**Daily Reflections to Strengthen
Your Faith**

Tiffany Nicole

ROCKRIDGE
PRESS

Interior and Cover Designer: Gabe Nansen
Art Producer: Megan Baggott
Editor: Brian Sweeting
Production Editor: Jael Fogle
Production Manager: David Zapanta

Paperback ISBN: 978-1-63878-726-6

R0

It is my honor to dedicate this book to you, the readers, who will be blessed by your commitment in taking the time to seek the Lord in your life. May you grow closer to Jesus and lean on His understanding and wisdom in every area of life.

INTRODUCTION

Hello and welcome to the next 90 days of building and strengthening your relationship with Jesus! I first want to congratulate you for taking the first step of saying YES to this devotional journal. This tells me that you are prioritizing your relationship with the Lord, and you desire to get to know Him in deeper and more intimate ways. My name is Tiffany, and I am the voice behind this devotional journal! I have the great privilege of leading you through the next 90 days where I will share my wisdom, failures, lessons learned, and insights into God's Holy Word.

Because women are such unique creations, we need a devotional specifically for us that speaks to our hearts, thought processes, and desires. In this devotional you will find encouraging verses that not only help you in your walk with the Lord, but also speak about who you are in Christ and what God says about you. We'll discuss various topics, such as how to mend difficult relationships, what to do when you begin to lose hope, and how to deal with stress and anxiety in a healthy way.

This devotional is tailor-made for the Christian woman with real advice, wisdom, and counsel on strengthening your relationships with the Lord and with other people. Although these devotions can be done at your leisure, I recommend you do them consecutively. Try to dedicate a specific time every day to this devotional, whether that be first thing in the morning or any other time of day. Just make sure you choose a time that is consistent and when you have a moment to yourself to fully engage and self-reflect. Last, I want to encourage you to be open and vulnerable with your responses to the journal prompts. Yes, it can be uncomfortable, but when you allow yourself to be vulnerable with yourself and God, that's when the real break-through happens. Amen? Okay, let's start!

God Is Always with You

So do not fear, for I am with you; do not be dismayed, for I am your God. I will strengthen you and help you; I will uphold you with my righteous right hand.

—Isaiah 41:10

When I first came to the Lord, hearing this verse about how God is with me absolutely broke me. Why? Because it seemed too good to be true. As an unbeliever, I felt very much alone when it came to my emotional pain and struggles. But after I read this verse, I knew that I would never again be alone. I serve a God who is always with me. Even though I can't see or touch Him, I know He's there. Through life's ups and downs, we have the comfort of knowing that our God is always with us.

Even after reading a verse like this one, we might still feel alone, even though we know we're not. If you ever feel alone, declare God's Word over you: "I have no reason to fear because God is always with me, even if I may not feel His presence." How does that affect how you feel?

My Best Friend, Jesus

*I no longer call you servants, because
a servant does not know his master's
business. Instead, I have called you friends,
for everything that I learned from my
Father I have made known to you.*

—John 15:15

Have you ever thought of Jesus as your friend? Many of us think of Him as our Lord or Savior, but He is also very much our friend. In fact, you were made for friendship with God. His desire is for you to do life with Him, so that everything you do is filtered through the lens of your relationship with Jesus. Just as God walked with Adam and Eve in the garden, He also desires to walk with you through every aspect of life—not just to know about God, but to know Him personally as a friend.

It can be challenging to view Jesus as your friend, especially if you're used to thinking of Him as Lord, Savior, and King. What aspects of viewing Jesus as your friend might you struggle with? How does knowing Jesus as a friend reshape your relationship with Him?

_____

_____

_____

_____

_____

_____

_____

_____

_____

_____

_____

_____

To Know &
Be Known

You have searched me, Lord,
and you know me.

—Psalm 139:1

Every human heart desires to be fully known, flaws and all, and to still be fully loved. Something that forever changed me was the realization that God knows me more than I even know myself. I'd spent my life feeling like I needed to explain myself to God, as if He had no clue what was going on in my life. But I had it wrong: God already knew everything about me. If you ever feel invisible or misunderstood, imagine God whispering in your ear, telling you that even when no one else understands you, He does. You are fully known by Him.

Sometimes all we want is to be understood—for someone to look into our heart and see what no one else can see. How does it feel knowing that God knows you? When you learned this, how did it change the way you view Him?

_____

_____

_____

_____

_____

_____

_____

_____

_____

_____

_____

The Truth About Trust

Trust in the Lord with all your heart and lean not on your own understanding; in all your ways submit to Him, and He will make your paths straight.

—Proverbs 3:5–6

For the longest time, I had an "I can do it alone" attitude. I thought I didn't need anyone, because it seemed like everyone I let in eventually let me down. I couldn't trust people, so I kept everyone at an arm's distance—including God. Trust me when I say it's not the way to live. We can't let our past pain with friends and family affect our relationship with the Lord. People will let you down, but God never will. If there's anyone you can trust, it is, and will always be, Jesus.

Our relationships with people tend to affect our relationship with God. That's why it's important that we let the Word of God trump how we feel, and let it stand as divine truth. What past experiences have shaped your ability to trust the Lord? If you sometimes resist trusting God, why do you think that is?

_____

_____

_____

_____

_____

_____

_____

_____

_____

_____

_____

Love Has a Name

Dear friends, let us love one another, for love comes from God. Everyone who loves has been born of God and knows God. Whoever does not love does not know God, because God is love.

—1 John 4:7-8

Many people think love is merely a feeling. We use the word love to refer to the warm, fuzzy feelings we have toward our partner, children, friends, or family members. However, the Bible tells us that love is actually a person. 1 John 4:8 says, "God is love," which means that although we can experience love as a feeling or an emotion, it is actually a person by the name of Jesus. Thus, as we draw closer to Jesus, we can't help but gain a greater understanding of what love truly is, because love is defined by God's very nature.

If you really want to understand love—where it comes from and how it works—talk to the person who defines Himself as love. Write down three things you love—anything from a person to a job. In what ways could you show Christ's love more, whether through your words or by your actions?

_____

_____

_____

_____

_____

_____

_____

_____

_____

_____

A Woman to Be Praised

Charm is deceptive, and beauty is fleeting;
but a woman who fears the Lord is
to be praised.

— Proverbs 31:30

This verse comes at the last section of the infamous Proverbs 31 passage, which talks of a woman of noble character. The Scripture leaves you with one defining trait from which every other godly female trait springs forth: A godly woman is one who fears the Lord. This type of fear refers to a woman who is completely in awe of God! She is a woman who trusts the Lord above the pressures of the world, the opinions of others, and even her own thoughts and feelings. She is a woman who has surrendered her life to Christ, putting His will first, above even her own.

Remember, a woman who fears the Lord is to be praised! It can be easy to become complacent in our relationship with the Lord. What are some things you do to maintain a reverent fear of the Lord?

_____

_____

_____

_____

_____

_____

_____

_____

_____

_____

She Laughs Without Fear of the Future

*She is clothed with strength and dignity;
she can laugh at the days to come.*

—Proverbs 31:25

God has created woman with wonderful gifts and abilities,
to be a blessing to her family, community, and workplace. As
this verse says, a truly godly woman is clothed in strength and
dignity, because she trusts in God with all her heart. She draws
her strength from the Lord and holds her head high because
she knows her value and worth as a daughter of God. She is not
afraid of the future but instead can be optimistic and hopeful for
what lies ahead, because she knows that God is always in control
and she has nothing to fear.

It's so easy to fall into doubt and worry. This proverb paints for us a picture of a woman who is fearless because of her trust in the Lord. When you think of the future, what feelings arise in you? How can trusting God enable you to look into your future without fear?

_____

_____

_____

_____

_____

_____

_____

_____

_____

_____

_____

_____

Household Heroes

She watches over the affairs of her household and does not eat the bread of idleness.

—Proverbs 31:27

Let's just say the Proverbs 31 woman wasn't spending her days mindlessly scrolling through social media and binge-watching TV shows. This woman knew that her role—in this case, as a homemaker and wife—was a blessing from the Lord, and she crushed it in fulfilling her kingdom assignment. Laziness was hardly part of her vocabulary; she was too busy managing the affairs of her home and not eating "the bread of idleness." Whether you're called to be a homemaker, a marketplace superstar, or something else, this proverb celebrates the woman who approaches her day mindfully and with purpose.

This verse isn't suggesting that you need to be "super-woman"; it's encouraging you to be thoughtful about how you manage your time. This could mean saying no if you tend to overextend yourself, or simply being more mindful about your current responsibilities. What are some areas where you might have taken on too much responsibility?

More Precious Than Rubies

A wife of noble character who can find?
She is worth far more than rubies.

—Proverbs 31:10

For centuries, rubies have been regarded as one of the world's most valuable gemstones for their distinct color and extreme rarity. Kings wore rubies in biblical times, and this gemstone has long been a symbol of wealth and power; it's also considered the "stone of love," evoking feelings of desire and passion. Yet, when it comes to finding a woman of noble character, the Bible says a woman who puts her faith and trust in the Lord is worth far more than rubies because of the godly traits living within her. This is a woman who is rare and valuable, and she should be cherished as such.

It's easy to forget our worth as daughters of God when we encounter those who don't value the things of God as a priority. However, women who love the Lord are extremely valuable. How does knowing your true worth in Christ affect the way you view yourself?

_____

_____

_____

_____

_____

_____

_____

_____

_____

_____

_____

DAY 10

Guard Your Heart

Above all else, guard your heart, for everything you do flows from it.

—Proverbs 4:23

Guarding your heart is one of the greatest things you can do, not just as a woman of God, but as a human being. Think about it— everything we do flows from our heart. It's where our dreams, desires, and passions live. Every thought, word, emotion, and action flows from the life spring that is the temperature of our heart. If your heart is bitter toward someone, negative thoughts, words, and actions will spring forth. But if you guard your heart and protect it from toxic emotions and feelings, you'll have the peace of God that surpasses all understanding.

God stresses the importance of guarding your heart above all else because your heart is the source of everything you do. In what areas of your life do you feel challenged to guard your heart? What benefits do you foresee?

_____

_____

_____

_____

_____

_____

_____

_____

_____

_____

_____

God Is within Her, She Will Not Fall

God is within her, she will not fall; God will help her at break of day

—Psalm 46:5

This psalm is one of the most popular verses in the Bible for women, and for good reason: It's very powerful and encouraging. However, this verse is meant not just for women, but for the whole church. Psalm 46 is telling us that God is our refuge and strength in times of trouble, and God's people will not fall because He is ever present in the lives of those who seek His name. God is so close to you that He actually dwells within you—and those who put their trust in the Lord cannot be destroyed.

God declares Himself a constant strength and place of refuge for His people. Whatever life may bring your way, God is not just with you, but also within you. How is God a strong fortress in your life? What obstacles are you facing? How can you lean on His strength, not yours, more?

The Savvy Businesswoman

She considers a field and buys it; out of her earnings she plants a vineyard.

—Proverbs 31:16

If you initially thought the "Proverbs 31 woman" is all about the ideal homemaker, think again! This virtuous woman is also an entrepreneur and savvy businesswoman. The first part of this verse speaks to her careful decision-making: She "considers" her investments thoughtfully (and prayerfully) before making a choice. And once she sets her mind on a course of action, she carries out her plans with confidence, following through without hesitation. She carefully considers the options, makes a decision, and focuses on getting it done, regardless of obstacles.

This verse paints a picture of careful decision-making; however, when she has made a decision, she follows through on her plans. Think about a big decision you made recently. Are you happy with it, or do you wish you'd made a different choice? Write about why you think back on it this way.

_____

_____

_____

_____

_____

_____

_____

_____

_____

_____

You Are Made in the Image of God

*So God created mankind in His own image,
in the image of God He created them; male
and female He created them.*

—Genesis 1:27

The Bible says that when God created Adam and Eve, He created mankind in His own image, which includes both male and female genders. God is neither male nor female, but is described throughout the Bible as both genders. Sometimes the Bible describes God in terms often associated with masculine traits, such as strength, and other times with feminine characteristics, such as the image of a woman in labor (Isaiah 42:14). As women, we uniquely reflect God's image, which is beautiful, and something we should delight in. We serve a God who not only knows us individually as people, but also understands us uniquely as women.

I have peace in knowing that I can be my true self—which is a daughter of God. Describe an aspect of your life that would benefit from taking the perspective that you are uniquely and distinctly made in the image of God as a woman.

_____

_____

_____

_____

_____

_____

_____

_____

_____

_____

_____

You Are Fearfully & Wonderfully Made

I praise You because I am fearfully and wonderfully made; Your works are wonderful, I know that full well.

—Psalm 139:14

To be wonderfully made means that you were made to be separate, distinguished, or unique—God made you to be special. The word "fearfully" is the Hebrew word *yare*—the same word is used in the Bible to refer to having a "fear of the Lord." However, "fear" in this sense means having a deep respect and reverence for God, not being afraid of Him. When the psalmist says you are "fearfully and wonderfully made," they mean you are a wonderful creation, worthy of respect and reverence, who is made in the image of God.

Many of us have, at some point, seen ourselves as average, inadequate, or worse. If you've ever felt this way, you weren't seeing yourself the way God sees you, as His wonderful creation made in His image. Write down 10 things you like about yourself. What makes you special and unique?

_____

_____

_____

_____

_____

_____

_____

_____

_____

_____

_____

You Are God's Masterpiece

---

*For we are God's handiwork, created in
Christ Jesus to do good works, which God
prepared in advance for us to do.*

—Ephesians 2:10

Did you know that every human being is a masterpiece of God?
Think about it for a moment: With seven billion people on the
planet, there's no one else with your fingerprint or your retina
scan. You are unique. You're an original design. Diamonds are
expensive because they are rare, but you're not rare: You're the
only you that exists or will ever exist! That makes you priceless.
You are God's masterpiece, a priceless work of art. God created
you as His masterpiece, uniquely designed with specific gifts
and talents, so you can fulfill the good works He prepared for
you long ago.

You may experience self-doubt and insecurity sometimes; remember that you are God's masterpiece, and there's no one else in the world like you. What are some of the gifts and talents God has placed with you? Ask God to reveal how you can use them to fulfill your unique calling.

_____

_____

_____

_____

_____

_____

_____

_____

_____

_____

_____

God Doesn't Make Accidents

For You created my inmost being; You knit me together in my mother's womb.

—Psalm 139:13

The Bible speaks of how God created us long before we were physically born. In the psalm, David describes how God formed his innermost being long before birth, knitting him together in his mother's womb. No one is an accident, regardless of the circumstances they were born into. It's important to remember that you are a product of God's omnipotent handiwork. You are a loved, cherished, and valuable creation of God, made with care. The God of the universe doesn't make accidents; you were made on purpose, for a purpose.

This verse beautifully depicts the Lord our God as the originator of every life. Many of us wonder why we are here and what our purpose is. Can you think of a situation in which reading this verse would comfort you or change your perspective on the meaning God has placed on your life?

_____

_____

_____

_____

_____

_____

_____

_____

_____

_____

_____

Be Strong & Courageous

"Have I not commanded you? Be strong and courageous. Do not be afraid; do not be discouraged, for the Lord your God will be with you wherever you go."

—Joshua 1:9

God tells us throughout the Bible to be strong and courageous. God isn't using these words as some sort of biblical motivational speech to help us get in gear; instead, He's actually commanding us to be strong. He is impressing upon us that those who are in Christ Jesus truly have nothing to fear. Of course this doesn't mean that challenges won't come our way. They will. But like Joshua, we can stand on God's promise that when we turn to Him for guidance and wisdom, we will succeed.

God often requires us to be bold when all we want to do is shrink back and remain hidden. In what ways has God prompted you to be strong and courageous? Were you tempted to listen to your fear, or did you listen to the voice of God?

_____

_____

_____

_____

_____

_____

_____

_____

_____

_____

_____

Runaways

But Jonah ran away from the Lord and headed for Tarshish. He went down to Joppa, where he found a ship bound for that port. After paying the fare, he went aboard and sailed for Tarshish to flee from the Lord.

—Jonah 1:3

There are times when the Lord will tell us things we don't want to hear. That was the case with Jonah. The Lord asked Jonah to do something he simply didn't want to do so . . . he ran. Like Jonah, we also tend to run away from the Lord. Maybe we're not physically running away and boarding boats to faraway lands, but we are running away mentally from the things God is calling us to do. Even when we don't want to do something, we have to trust that it is for our good and the good of those around us when we listen to the Lord's voice and obey Him.

It might seem silly that Jonah thought he could run away from the Lord, but we may be doing the same thing— we just don't realize it. Can you think of a time when you wanted to run away from the voice of God? What did you do?

_____

_____

_____

_____

_____

_____

_____

_____

_____

_____

_____

Equal, but Different

Then the Lord God made a woman from the rib He had taken out of the man, and He brought her to the man. The man said, "This is now bone of my bones and flesh of my flesh; she shall be called 'woman,' for she was taken out of man."

—Genesis 2:22-23

When making Adam, God used the "dust of the ground" to form his body. In creating Eve, God used one of Adam's ribs. God is showing us that Adam and Eve are made from the same substance. They are equal in every way, just different. Eve bears the image of God, just like Adam does, but everything from her physical appearance to her hormonal makeup to her chromosome structure is different. She was not created to be the same as Adam, but she was created to be equal to him in every way.

It's important to know beyond a shadow of a doubt that God deems women equal to men in every way, just different in design. In what ways are you proud to be a woman? What aspects of your femininity do you love?

_____

_____

_____

_____

_____

_____

_____

_____

_____

_____

_____

She Helps Those in Need

She opens her arms to the poor and extends her hands to the needy.

—Proverbs 31:20

We are called to love other people because loving others is an expression of the overflow of love we've already received from our relationship with God. God asks us to "open [our] arms to the poor" because when we truly love God, we also desire to love people in a real and tangible way. Often this requires more than just praying for people (but don't stop doing that!) so don't be surprised if God asks you to show up for your neighbor by serving the needs of others and extending your hand to the less fortunate.

Jesus, the Son of Man, did not come to be served, but to serve (Matthew 20:28). As God's daughters, we have also been given the same purpose and calling. Perhaps you have felt God nudging you to serve others more within your community. How might you do so?

_____

_____

_____

_____

_____

_____

_____

_____

_____

_____

DAY 21

Blessed Is She Who Believes

"Blessed is she who has believed that the Lord would fulfill His promises to her!"

—Luke 1:45

This verse was spoken to Mary, the mother of Jesus, before she gave birth. God had given Mary the biggest promise and gift to the world: that through her womb, she would bear the expected Messiah, the Savior of the World. Talk about big promises! What strikes me the most about this verse is the emphasis on the word "believed." God speaks life-altering promises about our life, and if we take Him at His word and believe Him, we are blessed. It may sound easy, but it can be a challenge. For those who dare to believe, get ready to be blessed.

Who else loves this verse? What a blessing it is to believe in the promises of God. What promises has God been speaking over your life? Whether they seem relatively small or giant and overwhelming, write them down so you can record how God has promised He will move in your life.

_____

_____

_____

_____

_____

_____

_____

_____

_____

_____

_____

A Kindhearted Woman Gains Honor

A kindhearted woman gains honor, but ruthless men gain only wealth.

—Proverbs 11:16

This verse is a contrast between men and women that tends to paint women in a very good light and men in a rather poor light. However, what the writer, King Solomon, is saying here isn't that all (or most) women are kindhearted or that all (or most) men are ruthless. He means a godly, gracious woman and a ruthless, aggressive man both gain something of value through their life choices and actions. While a ruthless man may gain wealth, gaining honor through showing kindness is much more valuable in the sight of God. Riches might be good, but gaining honor is far better.

God knows that many of His daughters desire security in the form of wealth and prosperity, but He wants us to know that honor and respect are far more desirable. Are you intentional about being kind to those around you? Describe a few ways you can show kindness more.

_____

_____

_____

_____

_____

_____

_____

_____

_____

_____

_____

Lady Wisdom

Out in the open wisdom calls aloud, she raises her voice in the public square; on top of the wall she cries out, at the city gate she makes her speech: "How long will you who are simple love your simple ways? How long will mockers delight in mockery and fools hate knowledge?"

—Proverbs 1:20–22

This verse! Don't you just love the drama of it all? After all, the book of Proverbs is a poem, and like all good poems it's chock-full of emotion, depth, and hidden meaning. You might have also noticed that throughout Proverbs, wisdom is personified as a woman. I dare say it's not because we're stereotyped as being emotional and dramatic. On the contrary, Proverbs describes Lady Wisdom as a woman who has much to offer—including wealth, honor, and righteousness (Proverbs 18-20)—to anyone who heeds her words. She's someone to be listened to, because her words offer the keys to living a successful life.

We all desire to live a successful life, but how many of us recognize that wisdom is the key to receiving it? The Bible says that God grants us wisdom when we ask. Write down three areas of your life in which you would like more of God's wisdom.

Be a Woman of Wisdom

*The fear of the Lord is the beginning of
wisdom, and knowledge of the Holy One
is understanding.*

—Proverbs 9:10

In the first nine chapters in the book of Proverbs we see Lady Wisdom contrasted with a young, foolish woman. The Bible advises us that if we want to be wise in how we live, it's best to listen to Lady Wisdom. In fact, Proverbs tells us that the beginning of true wisdom is having a godly fear of the Lord. This doesn't mean you should be afraid of God, but that you should have a deep respect and reverence for God. It means putting His will above your own, even when it's difficult and doesn't make sense, because you trust Him more than you trust yourself.

To fear the Lord is to live in awe of God—His sovereignty, goodness, mercy, and so much more. The Bible says that being in awe of God is the beginning of wisdom. Describe a time when you were in awe of God—maybe while enjoying a beautiful sunset or gazing at the stars.

How to Surpass Them All

"Many women do noble things, but you surpass them all."

—Proverbs 31:29

This verse comes toward the end of Proverbs 31, Virtuous Woman, and its placement is perfect. Verse 29 gives us much insight into how this fantastic female is able to do so much without becoming overwhelmed. The answer lies just before and after this quote that she is a woman of wisdom (v. 26) who fears the Lord (v. 30). She doesn't experience burnout because she trusts in the Lord in every endeavor He calls her to, and she wisely uses her skills to do that job well.

This verse encourages women to manage their time and to avoid overextending themselves to the point of exhaustion. Being organized, disciplined, and efficient might not come easily to everyone and can take some thoughtful effort. Can you think of five ways you could be wiser with the time that you have each day?

_____

_____

_____

_____

_____

_____

_____

_____

_____

_____

DAY 26

Speak With Wisdom

*She speaks with wisdom, and faithful
instruction is on her tongue.*

—Proverbs 31:26

In the book of Proverbs, Lady Wisdom describes herself as someone who has a lot to say, if only people would listen (Proverbs 1:20–33). Those who listen to her are promised a life that most people long for, one that includes health, wealth, and honor to their name. And just as Lady Wisdom speaks wisdom, Proverbs 31:26 also describes a woman who speaks wisdom and instruction to others. This tells me that when a woman hears and applies wisdom and instruction from the Lord, her words will also spring forth wisdom and instruction to bless anyone willing to listen.

Wisdom is speaking to you—are you listening? For you to speak wisdom yourself, you must first heed and apply God's wisdom and instruction. What kind of wisdom has God been speaking over you lately? How can you apply it to your life so you can speak it over others?

_____

_____

_____

_____

_____

_____

_____

_____

_____

_____

_____

DAY 27

The Hostess with the Mostest

She has prepared her meat and mixed her wine; she has also set her table.

Proverbs 9:2

Proverbs 9 reveals to us the difference between Wisdom and Folly, both personified as women who invite people to their homes for a meal. However, we see great contrasts between Wisdom's dinner party and Folly's. Folly is described as a seductive woman who entices people who walk past to come in and eat and drink her stolen bread and water, ultimately leading them to death. Wisdom, on the other hand, is the hostess with the mostest. She lavishes her guests with a table full of the finest foods and wine, symbolic of walking in the ways of the Lord, which leads to life.

54

It's through Jesus's teachings that we can become a wise spiritual "dinner host" for others, sharing our wisdom and insight with those around us. God is always presenting us with opportunities to do so. Have you ever had an opportunity to share your faith or Biblical wisdom with others? What happened?

_____

_____

_____

_____

_____

_____

_____

_____

_____

_____

_____

Unshakable Ground

"*Therefore everyone who hears these words of mine and puts them into practice is like a wise man who built his house on the rock. The rain came down, the streams rose, and the winds blew and beat against that house; yet it did not fall, because it had its foundation on the rock.*"

—Matthew 7:24–25

In this parable, Jesus tells a story about two men: one who builds his house on a rock and the other, who builds his on sand. (If you think Jesus's message was about house construction and building code violations—think again.) The meaning behind Jesus's words is that a proper foundation is necessary for building a house, and it's also true for building your life. When we live our lives in accordance with Jesus's words, and put them into practice, we're like the wise man who builds his house on solid, unshakable ground.

The proper foundation for our life comes from following the life and teachings of Jesus Christ. Each day, as we endeavor to follow God's Word, we're laying bricks that create a solid foundation of faith in our lives. What are three ways you can put into practice Jesus's teachings so you can build your life on unshakeable ground?

True Love Gives Sacrificially

Then Mary took about a pint of pure nard, an expensive perfume; she poured it on Jesus' feet and wiped His feet with her hair. And the house was filled with the fragrance of the perfume.

—John 12:3

This story focuses on a God-fearing woman, Mary, who gives up something precious to her in a beautiful act of love and worship of Jesus. The Bible says the perfume was worth a year's wages, and it likely represented her life savings and source of financial security. However, to Mary, Jesus was worth more than expensive perfume or financial security. In an act of love, she poured the perfume on Jesus's feet, wiping the oil with her hair. Just like Mary's devotion to Jesus resulted in a fragrant aroma, our love expressed to Jesus sends a fragrant aroma to the Lord.

Wiping someone's feet was a degrading act in Jewish culture. However, Mary performed this humble act, and gave up something precious to her, to show her love and devotion to the Lord. Many believers fast as a way to show their love and devotion, to draw closer to the Lord. What have you laid at the feet of Jesus as an act of love and devotion?

_____

_____

_____

_____

_____

_____

_____

_____

_____

_____

_____

DAY 30

Invitations & Promises

Come near to God and He will come near to you.

—James 4:8

The call to draw near to God is both an invitation and a promise. God's promise to us is that He will draw near to us as we draw near to Him. This speaks to the nature of God. He doesn't force anything, but gives us free will. He will not try to make you follow Him, love Him, or worship Him; instead He desires that you simply choose Him. The promise here is that when you do choose Him, He will lovingly reciprocate by drawing close to you.

Our faith in Jesus Christ is a relationship, not a religion. When you draw closer to God, you are getting to know a person who thinks, speaks, reasons, understands, and has feelings, just like you. How can you draw closer to God? How do you connect with Him the best?

_____

_____

_____

_____

_____

_____

_____

_____

_____

_____

_____

Daughters of the King

> *"I will be a Father to you, and you will be my sons and daughters, says the Lord Almighty."*
>
> —2 Corinthians 6:18

Have you ever thought of yourself as a daughter of the King? The Bible talks about God being our Father and also our King (Revelation 19:16). So, if God is both our Father and our King, we are daughters of the King. This truth speaks to our sense of worth and value as women. Many of us struggle at times with feeling unworthy, undervalued, or unloved—but the opposite is true! God tells us throughout the Bible that we're actually incredibly worthy, valuable, and loved. Proof of this love is Jesus's sacrifice on the cross, which gives us standing as daughters in God's Kingdom.

Remember that you are a daughter of the King! How does acknowledging this affect the way you view yourself? What situation or circumstance in your life is helped or enriched by knowing this?

Back on Track

"*Pick me up and throw me into the sea,*" *he replied, "and it will become calm. I know that it is my fault that this great storm has come upon you.*"

—Jonah 1:12

Jonah is known as the person in the Bible who tried to run away from God. Like Jonah, sometimes we resist the will of God in our life, choosing our own direction. My own Jonah story involves me moving to another country to live with my boyfriend at the time. I knew that living with my boyfriend wasn't God's will for my life, but I chose my own path anyway. The good news is that God is always with us, regardless of the decisions we make. As He did for Jonah, God provided a way for me to get back on track, and He will do the same for you.

Describe a time when you consciously ran away from the will of God. How did the Lord provide a way for you to get back on His path?

_____

_____

_____

_____

_____

_____

_____

_____

_____

_____

_____

You Are Blessed

Praise be to the God and Father of our Lord Jesus Christ, who has blessed us in the heavenly realms with every spiritual blessing in Christ.

—Ephesians 1:3

When I was going through a really tough season, I cried out to God with all of my pain and frustration about how awful my life seemed. To my surprise, I heard the Father say back, "Tiffany, you are blessed." I couldn't believe it. With everything I was going through, how could God consider me blessed? But after prayer and contemplation, I realized that "blessed" is my status as a believer in Jesus. It's not something I have to strive for; it's something I already have. Because we are daughters of the King, we are blessed.

You are blessed, regardless of any obstacle you may be facing. How does acknowledging that you are blessed just as you are, without any changes, affect the way you view yourself?

Dare to (Not) Compare

*We do not dare to classify or compare
ourselves with some who commend
themselves. When they measure
themselves by themselves and compare
themselves with themselves,
they are not wise.*

—2 Corinthians 10:12

Comparison can act like a poison, robbing you of satisfaction and contentment in who you are and the gifts God has given you. The greatest antidote for comparison is to remind yourself that God created you specifically and uniquely for a purpose. When you compare yourself negatively with others, you're telling yourself that you're not enough. But the truth is, you are enough. God has already given you everything you need for the plans and purposes He has set before you. Try not to measure yourself against others; instead, thank God for what you've been given, and steward it well for the Kingdom.

When we compare ourselves with others, we may feel that we don't measure up. Describe an aspect of your life that you think would benefit from a shift in perspective offered by today's devotional.

_____

_____

_____

_____

_____

_____

_____

_____

_____

_____

_____

_____

The Proper Way to Prosper

A generous person will prosper; whoever refreshes others will be refreshed.

—Proverbs 11:25

Sometimes we may feel that what we have is not enough. These thoughts can lead to feelings of envy, which create negative feelings toward even the best things in your life. If you find yourself feeling this way, remember that the opposite of envy is generosity. Proverbs 11:25 tells us that a generous person will prosper. This means when you bless others with your love and generosity, you will prosper in return, because the blessings you give others will come back to you in equal (and often greater!) measure.

Giving financially to others isn't the only way you can show generosity. Write down three ways you can be a more generous person.

_____

_____

_____

_____

_____

_____

_____

_____

_____

_____

_____

_____

Live for an Audience of One

Am I now trying to win the approval of human beings, or of God? Or am I trying to please people? If I were still trying to please people, I would not be a servant of Christ.

—Galatians 1:10

A people pleaser is someone who needs to be needed by others. It goes beyond personal desire for approval. People pleasers shape their identity and sense of self-worth by how others perceive them. Trust me, it's truly liberating when you no longer seek the approval and acceptance of others but instead strive to be a God pleaser: someone whose primary motivation is to please God. When you live your life for an audience of one, you shape your sense of self-worth around your identity as a daughter of God, not around the opinions of others.

Determining the difference between pleasing God and pleasing people boils down to a heart check. Take an inventory of five activities you're involved in. What is your motivation for participating? Are you aiming to please God or to please people?

Kingdom Perspective

*Your kingdom come, Your will be done,
on earth as it is in heaven.*

—Matthew 6:10

Having a Kingdom perspective means having a God perspective—meaning viewing life through God's lens, not your own. It's easy to get wrapped up in building our own little kingdoms (family, church groups, financial success) and lose touch with what is ultimately important to God: building the Kingdom of God here on Earth. Of course, God does care about the details of your life, including your family, church group, and financial success. However, keeping a Kingdom perspective means allowing God to be a part of every aspect of your life, putting Him first in everything you do.

A woman prays fervently to be accepted to a certain school but doesn't get in. She's initially disappointed, but she asks God to reveal to her what He is doing in her life. This is a Kingdom perspective. Think of three areas of your life right now and consider how you can have a Kingdom perspective on them.

_____

_____

_____

_____

_____

_____

_____

_____

_____

_____

_____

Seek First the Kingdom

But seek first His kingdom and His righteousness, and all these things will be given to you as well.

—Matthew 6:33

The Kingdom of God is the sovereignty of God and His rule over all creation. Jesus had more to say about the Kingdom of God than pretty much any other topic—this indicates how important seeking the Kingdom of God is. The word "seek" here refers to seeking God continually, without stopping. The beauty in seeking God's Kingdom is that you're getting to know a person, thus growing in your relationship with Jesus. Every day, you're given the opportunity to get to know Jesus the person in a deeper and more intimate way.

Jesus encourages us to seek God's Kingdom first, before anything else. How can you seek God more in your everyday life? Spending more time in prayer is a good start, but what about beyond that? One idea is to spend more time in silence, waiting on the Holy Spirit to speak to you.

Inner Beauty

Your beauty should not come from outward adornment, such as elaborate hairstyles and the wearing of gold jewelry or fine clothes. Rather, it should be that of your inner self, the unfading beauty of a gentle and quiet spirit, which is of great worth in God's sight.

—1 Peter 3:3-4

Audrey Hepburn said, "True beauty in a woman is reflected in her soul. It's the care that she lovingly gives, the passion that she shows." That's exactly what this verse is saying. A woman's true source of beauty is her inner self, not her appearance. Elaborate hairstyles, gold jewelry, and fine clothes can be lovely, but what people will remember about you is the way you treat them and how you make them feel. True beauty is displayed through love, gentleness, kindness, forgiveness, and peace. This kind of beauty doesn't fade away; instead, it's cultivated over time and becomes even more beautiful.

A woman who displays inner beauty is even-tempered and quick to forgive. She shows kindness and grace, and brings love and joy wherever she goes. What are three ways you can cultivate more inner beauty (love, joy, forgiveness, kindness) in your life? How can you share it with those around you?

Worthy of Respect

*In the same way, the women are to
be worthy of respect, not malicious
talkers but temperate and trustworthy
in everything.*

—1 Timothy 3:11

This verse was written about an elder's wife, but it applies to all of us regardless of our season of life and whether we're partnered or single. In the words of Paul the Apostle, Christian women should be women of respect, meaning women of integrity. A woman of integrity is someone other women can look up to, take counsel from, and follow as an example of how to be godly. However, we can't demand respect; instead, it must be earned. The way we earn respect from others is by being trustworthy and faithful in all things.

None of us like to be talked about behind our back or to have someone pass on something we shared in confidence. To gain trustworthy friends, we need to be a trustworthy friend first. Write down a few ways you can be a faithful and trustworthy friend.

_____

_____

_____

_____

_____

_____

_____

_____

_____

_____

_____

DAY 41

Lessons on Loyalty

But Ruth replied, "Don't urge me to leave you or to turn back from you. Where you go I will go, and where you stay I will stay. Your people will be my people and your God my God."

—Ruth 1:16

This powerful verse emphasizes the significance of loyalty. In the book of Ruth, Ruth's mother-in-law, Naomi, has lost her husband and two sons, leaving her a childless widow. Naomi urged the wives of her sons to return home and remarry, but Ruth refuses to leave her mother-in-law, declaring, "Where you go I will go, and where you stay I will stay." By saying this, Ruth meant that Naomi was now her home, and because God had brought them together, she would not abandon her. Ruth and Naomi put their trust in God. Because of their faith, God redeemed them—even making Ruth the great-grandmother of the greatest king in Israel, King David.

I can relate to Ruth's statement of loyalty. Following Jesus isn't always easy, but I find myself saying, "Wherever you are, God, that's where I want to be." Describe a situation or person where you were tempted to give up, but instead you remained loyal. What was the outcome?

_____

_____

_____

_____

_____

_____

_____

_____

_____

_____

_____

Let Your Light Shine

"You are the light of the world."

—Matthew 5:14

Jesus is calling each of His followers to be the light of the world! This means the presence of those who are believers in Jesus Christ should shine and bring about an atmosphere of encouragement, hope, and love. This doesn't mean you can never have a bad day or funky mood (we are human after all). But we should have the understanding that because we love the Lord we are marked with the Spirit of God, whose presence makes the world a better place. Because of God's Spirit which dwells within us, where there is darkness, we are able to illuminate the world by shedding God's light.

God has given each of us the ability to shine His light into the world! Describe a situation where you could see how your presence changed the atmosphere of those around you. What are three ways that you can shine God's light brighter?

_____

_____

_____

_____

_____

_____

_____

_____

_____

_____

_____

_____

A Life at Peace

If it is possible, as far as it depends on you,
live at peace with everyone.

—Romans 12:18

It takes two people to have a conflict, and it also takes two people to reconcile and live at peace. This can be frustrating sometimes, because you may be making valiant efforts to live amicably and at peace, but if the other person decides to hold a grudge or have an attitude, there's still strife in the relationship. Although you can't determine what another person says or does, you can choose to live at peace by controlling your own words and actions.

We are called to live at peace with everyone by being careful with our words, choosing our battles wisely, and being quick to forgive. Are you trying to live at peace with someone, but they've chosen to remain angry? Write a loving prayer for them, asking God to soften their heart.

_____

_____

_____

_____

_____

_____

_____

_____

_____

_____

_____

Small Beginnings

"Who dares despise the day of small things, since the seven eyes of the Lord that range throughout the earth will rejoice when they see the chosen capstone in the hand of Zerubbabel?"

—Zechariah 4:10

God has placed a purpose in everyone's life. Your goals may feel bigger than your capacity to achieve them, and that's okay. We're told to not despise the days of small beginnings. Instead, rejoice! The Lord loves to see the work begin. When the Lord first called me to start my blog and business, I felt like an imposter. I was discouraged when I spent so much time on a blog post and saw that only five people had read it (and four were family members!). Don't be discouraged by small beginnings. With hard work and the grace of God, you'll see your dreams come true.

What is something you feel the Lord has called you to begin? Write down five action steps you can take to move toward your larger goal that God has placed on your heart.

_____

_____

_____

_____

_____

_____

_____

_____

_____

_____

_____

_____

Be Still & Know

"Be still, and know that I am God; I will be exalted among the nations, I will be exalted in the earth."

—Psalm 46:10

This verse is a beautiful call to all believers who feel like they're in the middle of a battle, whether it be a relational, financial, emotional, or physical struggle. It's a reminder that we do not need to battle against the challenges we face with our own strength but can instead be still in the presence of God and rely on His unending power and strength. God is calling each of us to know who He is and to be in awe of Him. When we look at our situation with the true understanding of who God is, we know we have nothing to fear.

Each of us is called to be still and to know that God is Lord regardless of what we're facing. Maybe you're dealing with a physical illness, a conflict at work, or relationship challenges. How is God inviting you to shift your perspective by recognizing that with Him, you have nothing to fear?

_____

_____

_____

_____

_____

_____

_____

_____

_____

_____

_____

His Mercies Are New Every Morning

Because of the Lord's great love we are not consumed, for His compassions never fail. They are new every morning; great is Your faithfulness.

—Lamentations 3:22–23

The Bible says that God's mercies are "new every morning," meaning that God is unchanging and His love for us is steadfast and consistent. God keeps His promises, even when we don't. Think of every morning as a new beginning with God, where He demonstrates His unfailing grace toward us. When you arise each morning, remind yourself that every day is a new day, and God's mercies are there waiting for you. We may grow weary with the ups and downs of life, but God never does. He is an infinite source of compassion, grace, and mercy.

The love of God is unfathomable! God loves us uncondi-
tionally, showing us endless grace and mercy. In what ways
could you show others Christ's love more? Write down
three specific ways you can be more compassionate and
merciful to those around you.

_____

_____

_____

_____

_____

_____

_____

_____

_____

_____

_____

God Is Greater Than Your Problems

What, then, shall we say in response to these things? If God is for us, who can be against us?

—Romans 8:31

The question "Who can be against us?" is rhetorical. What the author is saying is, "There is no one who could possibly be more powerful than God!" I remember a season where it felt like absolutely nothing was working out no matter how hard I tried. All of my best efforts just lead to dead ends and it felt like my problems were greater than my God. But our feelings are not facts, which is why we have to always remind ourselves that Jesus is greater than our problems, worries, and greatest fears. It's not that we will never face challenges—we will, but our opposition's agenda will never be fulfilled, because our God is greater.

Despite these beautiful promises, when we're faced with financial, physical, mental, or emotional struggles, we might begin to wonder if God is truly for us. Describe a time when God showed you He was greater than your circumstance. Reflect on this story if you ever fall into doubt.

Drawing Closer

Who shall separate us from the love of Christ? Shall trouble or hardship or persecution or famine or nakedness or danger or sword?

—Romans 8:35

Paul, the author of the book of Romans, was very familiar with the hardships of life. He was imprisoned, stoned, beaten, and shipwrecked. Yet none of these events pulled him away from God. Instead, they drew Paul closer to Him. Through all of Paul's pain and despair, he actually became more familiar with the love of God, not less. If you're experiencing a difficult time, know that God is not watching from a distance, hoping you'll make it through. Instead, He's drawing closer to you, shielding you with the armor of His love so you can endure the battle.

Psalm 34:18 says that God is close to the brokenhearted. During difficult times, you're actually closer to God's love. Can you think of a painful experience that brought you closer to the Lord? Describe how you felt God's presence more strongly in that season. What did the comfort of God feel like?

_____

_____

_____

_____

_____

_____

_____

_____

_____

_____

More Than Conquerors

No, in all these things we are more than conquerors through Him who loved us.

—Romans 8:37

Many of you have probably heard that you are "more than conquerors" in Christ Jesus. Sounds amazing, right? But this isn't just a feel-good verse; being more than a conqueror in Jesus Christ means that no one can ever stop the power of God at work in your life. No struggle you'll ever face will be greater than the love of God. He will enable you to overcome every obstacle and actually come out the other side stronger from it.

Paul wrote the book of Romans to remind believers who they are in Jesus. When we forget who we are, we can be led to forget our power and authority in Christ. What obstacles are you facing? Write a note to yourself highlighting how strong you are because of your faith in Christ.

Walk the Walk

---

*Just as Christ was raised from the
dead through the glory of the Father,
we too may live a new life.*

—Romans 6:4

As Christians, we frequently say that when you come to Christ you are now "walking" with Jesus. But how exactly do you walk with Jesus? We walk with Jesus by changing the way we conduct, or live, our life by implementing the teachings of Jesus into our life. Now, this process isn't exactly easy. As you begin to walk out the teachings of Jesus, think of yourself as a toddler learning how to walk. Your legs might still be a bit wobbly because you aren't strong yet, but with practice you will get stronger and stronger until you grow into a mature Christian.

The joy of being a believer is that we get to walk with Jesus every day! Describe three things that God has shown you recently as you've walked with Him through life. How have you been implementing them into your life?

_____

_____

_____

_____

_____

_____

_____

_____

_____

_____

_____

DAY 51

The Key to Contentment

---

*I am not saying this because I am in need,
for I have learned to be content whatever
the circumstances.*

—Philippians 4:11

What Paul is telling us in this verse is that true contentment lies in a life rooted in Christ. The reason for this contentment is not based on your circumstances but is instead based on a person: Jesus. Now, contentment doesn't mean you stop desiring more for your life, such as a better job or a financial blessing. But it does mean you stop relying on having those things in order to be satisfied or fulfilled. The reality is, if you have Jesus and nothing else, then you have more than enough, because the power of Christ in your life will always be enough.

Life can be uncertain, but one thing we can hold onto is certainty in our faith in Jesus Christ. Write down three things that you desire in your life. What are some practical ways you can remain content in the wait, knowing that in Christ you already have all you need?

_____

_____

_____

_____

_____

_____

_____

_____

_____

_____

_____

With Christ, I Can Do All Things

I can do all this through Him who gives me strength.

—Philippians 4:13

Many think of this verse in the context of, "I can do whatever I set my mind to because of Christ who is my strength!" Instead, think of it more like, "No matter what I face, whether good or bad, I can overcome it because of Christ who is my strength." See the difference? Because of our faith in Jesus, there is a strength and confidence that rises up within us allowing us to be overcomers even among the most difficult circumstances and bleakest situations. As believers we have been equipped to be overcomers, not because of our own strength and ability, but because of Christ, who is our strength!

We are reminded to keep our eyes on Jesus, no matter what. He is our strength and strong tower (Proverbs 18:10). What obstacles have you been facing lately? How does knowing that Christ is your strength help you feel more content?

God Can Handle Your Broken Heart

The Lord is close to the brokenhearted and saves those who are crushed in spirit.

—Psalm 34:18

We serve a God who truly cares about His children. He not only knows about our pain but actually experiences it with us in a close and intimate way. When I went through a painful divorce, I felt the presence of God around me in ways I can't explain. As I was experiencing feelings of betrayal and disappointment, I knew that Jesus was with me through it all. He has an unending supply of empathy and comfort for us and isn't afraid to walk right up to the details of our situation and speak love and life into the most broken, discouraged, and painful areas of our life.

You may not realize it, but God is closest to you in your pain. You may not have a goosebump showing His presence, but keep your eyes open to see how God is showing up in your life. Think of five times that God has revealed Himself to you amid your pain.

Hope in Disappointment

But we had hoped that He was the one who was going to redeem Israel. And what is more, it is the third day since all this took place.

—Luke 24:21

Have you ever been disappointed by what you thought Jesus was doing in your life? Countless times, I thought my breakthrough was just around the corner—but it wasn't. Cleopas felt the same way. He spoke today's verse as he walked on the road to Emmaus with Jesus (completely unaware that he was talking to Jesus!). Cleopas expressed how he'd hoped that Jesus was the promised Messiah, the one to redeem Israel. But now Jesus was dead because He had been crucified. Of course, Cleopas didn't have the full story! His disappointment was short-lived; he later discovered that Jesus is the Messiah, the resurrection, and the life.

Sometimes things don't work out the way we'd hoped, but we can't give up! There's always hope in Jesus. Have you ever felt disappointed in Jesus? How does this story shift your perspective to see a bigger picture of what God is doing in your life?

Perfect Peace

Peace I leave with you; my peace I give you. I do not give to you as the world gives. Do not let your hearts be troubled and do not be afraid.

—John 14:27

The world offers a form of peace that is good, and trust me, I am thankful for it. The world's peace comes in the form of police officers, security systems, retirement plans, health insurance, etc., but Jesus's peace is different. Jesus offers a peace that is not circumstantially based. The peace of God is a peace that makes no sense! It's a feeling of security and comfort that you can still have despite bad circumstances, trials and tribulations, or heartbreak and loss. Even when life is throwing you the most ridiculous nonsensical garbage and nothing seems to be going right, you can still have Jesus's peace, which is the peace of God that transcends all understanding.

The peace of God is activated in your life when you truly believe that God is who He says He is. What's an area of your life you are troubled by or concerned about? Write a prayer asking God to give you His peace over that area.

_____

_____

_____

_____

_____

_____

_____

_____

_____

_____

_____

How to Determine God's Will

Then you will be able to test and approve
what God's will is—His good, pleasing
and perfect will.

—Romans 12:2

In today's verse, Paul tells us that we can actually test and confirm what God's will for our life is. This is exciting news! God doesn't desire for you to blindly go through life guessing at what His will is. Instead, God is leading and guiding you toward His good, pleasing, and perfect will. However, the key to knowing God's will is knowing God's Word. When you fill yourself up with God's Word, you will inevitably know God's will, because you are filling yourself with the truth of who God is. So, if you are unsure that a choice you are wanting to make aligns with God's will, first check God's Word and pray for wisdom, guidance, and clarity.

Knowing God's will for your life changes the way you behave, speak, and react. Think of three areas in your life where you're not sure about God's will. Search the Bible to find what the Word of God says on these subjects. Write what you've discovered.

_____

_____

_____

_____

_____

_____

_____

_____

_____

_____

_____

_____

_____

Blessed Is She Who Trusts in the Lord

"But blessed is the one who trusts in the Lord, whose confidence is in Him."

—Jeremiah 17:7

Telling someone to trust in the Lord is one of the easiest pieces of advice to give, but implementing that advice is hard. Trust me when I say even when you think you trust the Lord, you won't truly know for sure until you're put in a situation where you're forced to either stay faithful in what you believe or give in to fear and doubt. However, this verse says blessed is the woman who trusts in the Lord and places her confidence in Him. This means you are blessed when you take God at His Word and don't allow yourself to be shaken by your circumstances, feelings, and emotions.

It pleases the heart of God when His children depend on Him completely, believing in His Word and trusting in His promises. When was the last time you felt tested to trust completely in the Lord? What did you learn from that experience that you can put into use?

_____

_____

_____

_____

_____

_____

_____

_____

_____

_____

_____

You Are Who You Are

But by the grace of God I am what I am, and His grace to me was not without effect.

—1 Corinthians 15:10

Nearly all of us have felt like a misfit at one time or another. Many women secretly struggle with why they are the way they are. If we don't fit the mold of how we think a woman should behave, act, or feel, we can be left feeling like there's something wrong with us. But I'm here to tell you that God fashioned you perfectly for His calling and gifting in your life. Your differences make you unique—and God made you with certain characteristics and personality traits for the special calling He has for your life.

If everyone were alike, this world would be a lot less interesting! Make a list of 10 things that are unique about you, whether you've come to appreciate them or not. Describe how you can use these unique gifts to fulfill God's calling and purpose for your life.

_____

_____

_____

_____

_____

_____

_____

_____

_____

_____

_____

_____

God Has Not Given You a Spirit of Fear

For the Spirit God gave us does not make us timid, but gives us power, love and self-discipline.

—2 Timothy 1:7

God tells us repeatedly in His Word not to fear. The reason why we shouldn't fear is simply because God hasn't given us fear. Instead, God has given us His Spirit, which does the exact opposite of fear. Instead of making us fearful and timid, God's Spirit within us makes us powerful, loving, disciplined, and of a sound mind. From the inundation of negative reports on the news to family drama and tension, we are constantly presented with opportunities to choose fear over faith. But God's intention for His children is for us to be completely fearless people who are marked by our resilient faith and trust in Jesus Christ, free from doubt, worry, and discouragement.

We may experience fear, doubt, worry, and discouragement, but we overcome those feelings through the sustaining power of God's love. Describe a situation in which you were afraid to do something, but your faith in Jesus helped you overcome that fear and do it.

_____

_____

_____

_____

_____

_____

_____

_____

_____

_____

_____

God Has Plans for You

"For I know the plans I have for you,"
declares the Lord, "plans to prosper you
and not to harm you, plans to give you
hope and a future."
—Jeremiah 29:11

God has plans for you and they're great ones! When God sent this message to the prophet Jeremiah, Israel was being oppressed by Babylon and its people were being held in captivity. Yet God sent them this message of hope because despite how things appeared, He had plans for them that were for their good. In the same way, despite how things may look in your life, God has plans for you that are for your good. God doesn't promise us immediate rescue from our hardship, but He does promise us that He has plans for our life that are for welfare, goodness, and prosperity, not calamity, hardship, or evil.

God sent Israel this message when they needed a word of encouragement and hope for their future. As we journey through life, we also need encouragement and hope for our future. Describe a time in your life when you felt like you were ready to give up, but instead you received a word of encouragement and hope from the Lord.

_____

_____

_____

_____

_____

_____

_____

_____

_____

_____

_____

You Are Beautiful, My Darling

You are altogether beautiful, my darling; there is no flaw in you.

—Song of Songs 4:7

The Song of Songs is a poem dialoguing the love between a young woman and her lover. It explores the human experience of love and sexual desire with elaborate descriptions of their attraction and love for each other. If you were wondering what love poetry is doing in the Bible, you might be surprised to hear that this book has a twofold meaning. It is very much a love poem, but it's also a symbol of Christ's love for His people, the church, and how He looks upon you, His beloved. You are beautifully redeemed, completely flawless, without a spot or blemish.

Most of us do not always feel flawless, and we may feel frustrated with ourselves when we make a mistake. Describe how this verse can help you realize that God sees you as beautifully redeemed.

_____

_____

_____

_____

_____

_____

_____

_____

_____

_____

Trust—Even When It Doesn't Make Sense

*Trust in the Lord with all your heart and
lean not on your own understanding.*

—Proverbs 3:5

This is one of the most beautiful verses in the Bible, and one
that I gravitated toward even as a little girl. There's so much in
the world that I don't understand, and this verse reminds me
that's okay. I just need to trust God with all my heart and lean
on His understanding—He is the One who knows, sees, and is in
control of all things. Things may not make sense to me, but they
make perfect sense to God. When you don't have the answers,
lean on His wisdom and guidance to see you through the twists
and turns of life.

Learning how to truly trust God is a lifelong journey. What lessons have you learned about trusting in God throughout your life? Were there times when what you believed in didn't make sense? What has surprised you about the journey?

_____

_____

_____

_____

_____

_____

_____

_____

_____

_____

_____

Higher Love

"For my thoughts are not your thoughts, neither are your ways my ways," declares the Lord. "As the heavens are higher than the earth, so are my ways higher than your ways and my thoughts than your thoughts."

—Isaiah 55:8–9

Have you ever questioned God and thought, "Why didn't things turn out the way I'd hoped? Why is this happening to me?" We can struggle to trust a God we don't fully understand, and we become frustrated when we can't comprehend His ways. However, in this verse, God tells us that His thoughts are not our thoughts and His ways are not our ways. God's thoughts and ways are higher. They may not make sense to us, but we can rest in knowing that His ways are always good and He's working everything out for our good.

God's ways are higher than our ways! He sees things that we can't. Describe how this verse can help you trust God in an area of your life where you wish you had more insight and clarity.

_____

_____

_____

_____

_____

_____

_____

_____

_____

_____

_____

Really, It's All about Trust

In all your ways submit to Him, and He will make your paths straight.

—Proverbs 3:6

What this verse means is that God's best for you involves your full surrender. By giving every area of your life over to God, you allow Him to be a part of everything you do. At the end of the day, it's all about trust. God is wondering if you'll trust Him with your future and allow Him to direct your path. It's a heart posture that says, "Lord, I trust you with the plans of my life more than I trust myself, so I willingly submit my life into your trustworthy hands, believing that you know best."

Many of us struggle at times with surrendering our lives over to the Lord. Certain areas are easier to surrender than others. In which areas of your life is it easier to trust in God (for example, improving finances or finding a partner)? Which areas are harder?

Think Positive Thoughts

Finally, brothers and sisters, whatever is true, whatever is noble, whatever is right, whatever is pure, whatever is lovely, whatever is admirable—if anything is excellent or praiseworthy—think about such things.

Philippians 4:8

I remember the day I discovered today's verse. I exclaimed, "Oh my gosh, positive thinking is actually Biblical?!" I'd read scientific studies on the benefits of positive thinking, but my mind was blown when I discovered that the Bible recommended it thousands of years ago, long before neuroscientific studies on the subject. The Bible tells us that to be of sound mind, free from negative thoughts, fears, and anxiety, we need to think about things that are excellent or worthy of praise. When we focus on what is good, lovely, and admirable, God's peace, joy, and love will come over us, giving us a sound mind.

Many of us tend to focus on the negative things in our lives. Regardless of what you're going through, there's always something to be thankful for. Make a list of five things that bring you joy, and revisit this list whenever you feel negativity, fear, or anxiety coming over you.

_____

_____

_____

_____

_____

_____

_____

_____

_____

_____

_____

Forgiveness Is Healing

Therefore confess your sins to each other and pray for each other so that you may be healed.

—James 5:16

Have you ever wondered why the Bible speaks on forgiveness so much? The reason is that living in a place of unforgiveness keeps hurt, anger, and blame alive, tainting your perception of life and future relationships. When you forgive someone, you let go of that pain and anger instead of allowing it to eat at you. Some believe that forgiveness is a form of weakness or is equivalent to allowing an undeserving person to "win"—but it has zero connection to weakness, or even to emotions. Forgiveness is an act of will, and will can function regardless of the temperature of the heart.

Forgiveness will always lead you toward happiness, joy, and peace of mind and heart. Nearly all of us have someone we need to forgive. Who comes to mind for you? Write their name here, and compose a prayer asking the Lord to help soften your heart so you can forgive them.

_____

_____

_____

_____

_____

_____

_____

_____

_____

_____

_____

A Life in Harmony

*Finally, all of you, be like-minded,
be sympathetic, love one another,
be compassionate and humble.*

—1 Peter 3:8

In this verse, Peter is urging harmony within the church. Many of the early Christian churches experienced division and strife, just like many of us experience conflict today. Peter is encouraging healthy relationships and harmonious living within the body of Christ. To do this, he says, we should have unity in the way we think. We should be sympathetic to one another and love each other with humility and compassion. We do this is by being loving and quick to forgive, and not holding onto bitterness, despite one another's shortcomings.

My mom used to say, "Never judge someone until you've walked a mile in their shoes." You never know what someone is going through. Think of a time when you may have been quick to judge someone. How does this verse inspire you to be more loving and compassionate toward those around you?

Kindness Is King

Be kind and compassionate to one another, forgiving each other, just as in Christ God forgave you.

—Ephesians 4:32

It might seem surprising that the Bible has to tell us to be kind and compassionate to one another (then again, maybe not!). Have you ever been wronged by someone? The kind of wrong where you were really hurt? Our natural reaction might involve feelings of anger, bitterness, disappointment, and desire for revenge. This is human. We're made to have emotions, but it's what you do with your emotions that matters. When your heart is hurting, remember this verse. Instead of saying something hurtful, choose to show compassion, kindness, and love.

You can't control what someone has done to you, but you can control how you treat them in return. What is your natural reaction when you've been wronged? If you find it difficult to forgive, how can you practice kindness even when you think someone doesn't deserve it?

Clothed in Righteousness

*I put on righteousness as my clothing;
justice was my robe and my turban.*

—Job 29:14

Scripture often describes our behavior as the clothes we wear. On the cross, Jesus took off His "robe" of sinless perfection, and instead clothed Himself with our sin. An exchange occurred at the cross: Jesus wore our sin so we could wear His righteousness. Our sin was wiped away, and in its place we wear the righteousness of Christ. We are no longer defined by our weakest moments; instead, we are a new creation in Christ. The new "clothes" we wear are now a reflection of who we are in Christ: a righteous and holy daughter of the King.

Even though we've been clothed in righteousness, many of us struggle to see ourselves that way. Think of an area in your life where you still feel some shame or regret. Write a prayer asking God to help you see yourself the way He sees you: a holy, blameless, beautiful daughter of God.

_____

_____

_____

_____

_____

_____

_____

_____

_____

_____

_____

Something Worth Fighting For

Fight the good fight of the faith. Take hold of the eternal life to which you were called when you made your good confession in the presence of many witnesses.

—1 Timothy 6:12

I used to think "walking by faith" meant that I could effortlessly glide through life, but I realized that's not true. Living out our faith in Jesus requires a lot of effort. For example, we're instructed to forgive people who have hurt us deeply and to love others even when they are cruel. For many, this seems like an impossible ask. But Jesus promises us that what's impossible with people is possible with God (Luke 18:27). So, don't grow weary in walking out your faith. Continuing to live out the Christian faith, as difficult as it may seem at times, is something worth fighting for!

Describe a time when you felt challenged by the Bible or the Christian walk (see Walk the Walk, page 100). How did you overcome these challenges? What helped you push through and keep fighting for your faith?

Renew Your Mind

Do not conform to the pattern of this world, but be transformed by the renewing of your mind.

—Romans 12:2

Did you know that the Bible tells us we can actually change the way we think—or, as Romans 12:2 puts it, renew our mind? The process of renewing our mind is fascinating, because research has shown that our brains are neuroplastic, which means they can change continually over the course of our life. It takes an average of 21 days to break a bad habit and create a new, healthy one. So be patient with yourself! Each day, when you read Jesus's teachings and apply them to your life, imagine your brain creating new habits and behaviors.

Many of us struggle with negative thoughts and behaviors, but how exciting is it to know that you can actually change your behavior by changing the way you think? Write down the areas of your life you'd like to see transformed by the renewing of your mind.

_____

_____

_____

_____

_____

_____

_____

_____

_____

_____

_____

Biblical Blessings

Let us not become weary in doing good,
for at the proper time we will reap a
harvest if we do not give up.

I loved my grandma deeply, and shortly after she passed, I felt
God calling me to take an extended leave from work to help my
mother. I really wanted to be there for my mom, but stress and
emotions ran high, and sometimes I just wanted to leave. That's
when I felt the Lord speak Galatians 6:9 over me, telling me not
to grow weary in doing good. God was calling me to be there
for my mother, and although it was difficult at times, I knew
I couldn't grow weary in helping her. In time there would be a
harvest of blessing from our time spent together.

Sometimes God will call you to do something difficult, but don't give up! You never know what blessing God intends for you awaits on the other side. Describe a situation in which you grew weary in doing good, but your faith in Jesus helped you keep going.

God's Timing Is Not Your Timing

But do not forget this one thing, dear friends: With the Lord a day is like a thousand years, and a thousand years are like a day.

—2 Peter 3:8

Countless times, when I prayed for something and my prayer wasn't answered within the timing I'd hoped for, I experienced disappointment in my faith. I thought I was alone in this, but I realized I wasn't—the believers in the Bible experienced the same frustrations with the Lord's timing. In fact, this verse was written to explain that our timing is different from the Lord's. To the Lord, a day is like a thousand years, and a thousand years are like a day. This is a reminder to trust the timing of your life, because God knows what He's doing and is always in control.

Try not to be discouraged when things don't happen on your timetable. God is not limited by the same time constraints we are. Describe a prayer request that has yet to be answered. How do you feel when you acknowledge that God's timing is different from yours?

_____

_____

_____

_____

_____

_____

_____

_____

_____

_____

Hope in the Lord

No one who hopes in You will ever be put to shame.

—Psalm 25:3

Over the years, I've hoped for Jesus to do a number of things in my life, including providing financial security, a rewarding career, a godly husband, a family, and physical and emotional healing. Sometimes I felt a little silly placing my hope in Jesus for these things. The seductive voice of fear whispers in my ear, "You can't tell people you're believing in God for these things. If they don't happen, you'll be so ashamed and embarrassed." But no one who hopes in the Lord will ever be put to shame. Don't be afraid to place your hope in God. He can be trusted with your heart's deepest desires.

We honor God when we place our hope in Him. Describe a situation in which you were afraid to hope that Jesus would do something in your life. How does this verse help you feel more confident in the hope you have placed in Christ?

_____

_____

_____

_____

_____

_____

_____

_____

_____

_____

_____

I Can See Clearly Now

Jesus replied, "You do not realize now what I am doing, but later you will understand."

—John 13:7

Sometimes God will ask you to follow Him without a full understanding of what He is doing in your life. For example, some time ago the Lord called me to move to California from Virginia. It seemed ridiculous, but I couldn't shake the feeling that the Lord wanted me to move—so I did. Now that I'm settled, I have a greater understanding of why God called me to move. In the moment, we might not see clearly what God is doing in our lives, but give it time; later we will understand.

When we can't see, God asks us to trust Him that He can. Describe a time you didn't understand what God was doing in your life, but you trusted Him anyway.

God Will Supply Your Every Need

*And my God will meet all your
needs according to the riches of
His glory in Christ Jesus.*

—Philippians 4:19

It wasn't until I hit a rough financial patch that I truly understood the meaning of this verse. There were times when I didn't know if I would be able to cover my monthly bills, and that was scary. I did everything I could to make more money, but nothing seemed to be working. As uncomfortable as that time was, one thing I'm grateful for is that I was able to see this verse come to life around the area of my finances. Month after month, I saw God's favor and how He continued to provide for me, meeting all my needs.

Financial hardships may come our way, but we need to remember that God will supply our every need. How does acknowledging that God is your provider change the way you view your finances? Can you think of a time when you had to rely on God to supply your needs, financial or otherwise?

_____

_____

_____

_____

_____

_____

_____

_____

_____

_____

_____

Wait Patiently for the Lord

Be still before the Lord and wait patiently for Him.

—Psalm 37:7

Waiting on the Lord is quite possibly the hardest thing to do. It's a lesson in obedience and trust, believing that God will do what He says He will do. In Genesis 17, God promised Abraham a son even though he was 99 and his wife could not conceive. The promise was exciting, but the wait was . . . unbearable. After a staggering 25 years, baby Isaac was finally born! No matter the length of time, waiting is never easy. But don't settle for something quicker and easier—wait patiently for the Lord.

When you're in the waiting season, a month can feel like a lifetime. But Psalm 37:7 reminds us to wait patiently on the Lord and avoid getting discouraged. Describe an aspect of your life in which you've been waiting on the Lord. How does this devotional inspire you to patiently trust God?

_____

_____

_____

_____

_____

_____

_____

_____

_____

_____

_____

Train a Child in the Way He Should Go

Start children off on the way they should go, and even when they are old they will not turn from it.

—Proverbs 22:6

This is one of the most famous parenting verses in the Bible. This verse should be understood as a wise statement from the Lord offering us the best path and pattern to success. Christian parents, caretakers, educators, and other adults have a tremendous ability to impact children's belief systems by teaching them in the way of salvation through Jesus Christ. This doesn't mean forcing them into a certain set of belief systems, but leading by example by living out our own faith in Christ.

We are all called to be an example for children—whether we're parents or not—by leading them in the ways of the Lord. Write down three ways you can be an example to children in the Christian faith (for example, plan to volunteer with kids or teach them nightly prayers).

Cast Your Cares on the Lord

Cast all your anxiety on Him because He cares for you.

—1 Peter 5:7

Many aspects of life have the potential to overwhelm me, but thankfully, I know that with Jesus I don't have to tackle them alone. I can place all my burdens and anxiety on the Lord. By casting your cares on the Lord, you're relinquishing control and saying, "God, I can't even begin to fix this, but You can. I don't know how You'll do it, but I know that You can see me through." Regardless of what you're going through, nothing is too big or too difficult for God. Cast your cares onto Him, because He cares for you.

We cast our cares on the Lord by trusting Him with our problems. Many of us struggle with worry and anxiety, but when we trust God, we can have complete peace of mind. Describe an aspect of your life that you think would benefit from casting your anxieties on the Lord.

_____

_____

_____

_____

_____

_____

_____

_____

_____

_____

_____

Do Everything in Love

Do everything in love.

—1 Corinthians 16:14

What an amazing goal, to do everything in love. This verse is challenging, though. I believe the vast majority of us truly desire to love others well, but obstacles often seem to get in the way. Instead, we might find other emotions, such as anger, bitterness, or jealousy, rearing their ugly heads, tearing down the banner of love we wish to display. However, when we allow God to fill us up with His love, we will have an overflow of love that pours out in everything that we do.

Love is the core of the Christian faith, and 1 John 4:8 even tells us that God Himself is love. Write down three ways you can spend more time with God this week and be filled with His love. How does this shape your ability to do everything in love?

_____

_____

_____

_____

_____

_____

_____

_____

_____

_____

_____

_____

Love God with All Your Heart

Jesus replied: "'Love the Lord your God with all your heart and with all your soul and with all your mind.' This is the first and greatest commandment."

—Matthew 22:37-38

The call to love God with all your heart is something we all desire. But let's be honest: Although we love God, He's not the only one we love. So how can we obey this command when so many other things compete for our heart's affections? Well, the Lord is completely aware of our shortcomings. He tells us that our love for Him originates from His love for us: "We love because He first loved us" (1 John 4:19). As our understanding of God's love for us grows, we'll love Him more in return—fulfilling His greatest commandment.

God's love for us is actually the source of our love for Him. Because of His great love for us, we are infused with a love for Him. Can you think of a time when you felt overwhelmed by God's love for you? How did it impact your love for the Lord?

_____

_____

_____

_____

_____

_____

_____

_____

_____

_____

_____

Exceedingly & Abundantly

Now to Him who is able to do immeasurably more than all we ask or imagine, according to His power that is at work within us.

—Ephesians 3:20

I love this verse because it speaks to the wonder and awe of God. We tend to focus on our problems, allowing them to grow into giant mountains that feel impossible to climb. However, God is far bigger than anything we can imagine. Nothing is impossible for God! He can answer any prayer, perform any miracle, heal any sickness, and save even the most lost soul. When we fix our eyes on God and not on our problems, we realize that nothing is too difficult for the Lord. He can do immeasurably more than we can imagine—all we need to do is believe.

Nothing is greater than the power of our God. When you're praying, remember that you are praying to a God who is absolutely limitless. What are you believing God for in your life? Write down three specific ways you are actively praying for Him to move in your life.

_____

_____

_____

_____

_____

_____

_____

_____

_____

_____

_____

God Sings over You!

"He will take great delight in you; in His love He will no longer rebuke you, but will rejoice over you with singing."

—Zephaniah 3:17

The depth of God's love for us is hard for us to imagine, but this verse in Zephaniah reveals a breathtaking truth: God delights in us and rejoices over us with singing! Yes, singing! God loves us so much that He sings over us. Throughout the Bible, singing is a representation of God's joy, so when this verse says God rejoices over you, it literally means God dances, skips, leaps, and spins around with joy for you. That's how much God loves you—He is actually dancing and singing in delight over you!

God is pleased with you and delights in you! Sometimes we feel so burdened with the shame from our past that we forget about the wonders of God's love. Take a moment and imagine God singing and dancing over you. How does this image make you feel? Describe what you see.

Praise into His Presence

Enter His gates with thanksgiving and His courts with praise; give thanks to Him and praise His name.

—Psalm 100:4

Did you know that "entering into His gates" is synonymous with coming into the Lord's presence? When I realized this, it was a game changer. I realized that if I wanted to feel the presence of God more strongly in my life, I simply needed to thank Him and praise Him for who He is, what He's done in my life, and what He says He'll do in the future. If you struggle with intimacy with God or unanswered prayers, give Him praise. Don't wait for Him to answer your prayer to thank Him—do it in advance, because He is worthy of our praise.

I'll share a secret I've learned in my walk with the Lord: Starting my prayers with praise accelerates the level of intimacy I experience with Him. The Lord is pleased when we praise Him. Write down 10 things you're thankful for, and thank God for them during your quiet time with Him.

All Things New

*See, I am doing a new thing! Now it
springs up; do you not perceive it?
I am making a way in the wilderness
and streams in the wasteland.*
—Isaiah 43:19

The Lord is always saying to us, "See, I am doing a new thing!"
He's constantly calling us to rise out of the ordinary. If you feel
God calling you to do something you think you're completely
unqualified for, you just might be on the right track. The more
impossible the task seems, the more God will do exactly what He
says in this verse, and make a way in the wilderness and streams
in the wasteland. If you could do it yourself, you wouldn't need
God. God calls us to stretch our limits, so we can see His mighty
hand at work in us.

God is always doing new things in our lives, but sometimes we're not in tune and able to see them. Write down three things that God could be doing in your life to encourage you to stretch your limits and grow in your relationship with Him and His purpose for you.

_____

_____

_____

_____

_____

_____

_____

_____

_____

_____

_____

Promotion Comes from the Lord

So Samuel took the horn of oil and anointed him in the presence of his brothers, and from that day on the Spirit of the Lord came powerfully upon David.

—1 Samuel 16:13

Have you ever felt stuck in life? Like you're doing the right things but not getting anywhere? David must have felt that way throughout the book of 1 Samuel. He was anointed the next king of Israel as a teenager, but he wouldn't become king for nearly 15 years. During that time, he lived as an outlaw, on the run from King Saul. David must have questioned what was going on in his life. Your present circumstances, like David's, may not reflect the life you know you're capable of, but trust the process. Promotion doesn't come from other people, or even your best efforts—it comes from the Lord.

Even though David knew he would be king, for 15 years his life did not reflect this future. Describe a situation in which you felt discouraged because your reality didn't reflect the hopes and dreams in your heart. How does the story of David give you new hope?

Keep Your Eyes on Jesus

"Come," [Jesus] said. Then Peter got down out of the boat, walked on the water and came toward Jesus. But when he saw the wind, he was afraid and, beginning to sink, cried out, "Lord, save me!"

—Matthew 14:29–30

Many believers are constantly playing tug-of-war, going back and forth between depending on themselves and depending wholeheartedly on God. For example, when God called me to offer Christian coaching for women, initially I was terrified and I prayed constantly for strength. But after I became more confident, my reliance on the Lord loosened up, and my prayers became less frequent. Like Peter, when I took my eyes off the Lord, I began to sink. I realized that regardless of how successful I am, I must keep my eyes first on Him, relying on His strength.

Can you think of a time when you prayed incessantly for something that is now a normal part of your life? Maybe it's a job you wanted, a spouse, or a baby. Write a prayer asking God to create in you a life devoted to and reliant on Him, regardless of your circumstances.

_____

_____

_____

_____

_____

_____

_____

_____

_____

_____

DAY 88

Free from Shame

*Adam and his wife were both naked,
and they felt no shame.*

—Genesis 2:25

Shame can be summed up in one word: terrible. It's different from all other emotions, because instead of feeling like you've *done* something wrong, shame is the feeling of *being* something wrong. We think, "I'm too outgoing, I'm too quiet, I'm too heavy, I'm too thin, if only I were smarter, or more beautiful"—the list goes on. So how do you fix *being* something wrong? Thankfully, as believers in the gospel, we enjoy the universal remedy: Through His sacrifice on the cross, Jesus took on our sin so that we could live in perfect harmony with God again, free from all shame.

God's design is for us to be loved, free from all shame. Describe an aspect of yourself or your life that you didn't celebrate before, but now you love. What changed your view?

_____

_____

_____

_____

_____

_____

_____

_____

_____

_____

_____

Leaps of Faith

Now faith is confidence in what we hope for and assurance about what we do not see.

—Hebrews 11:1

The Bible is really interesting sometimes. In this verse, God encourages us to not depend on the things we see right in front of us, and instead to have faith in what we cannot see. Mark 11:24 even goes so far as to say that if we believe that we already have what we are praying for, it will be ours. Sounds unbelievable, right? But that's God's call for His people: for us to live by faith and not by sight. To trust in what is not yet seen, instead of what is seen.

The way we see God's promises come to fruition is by having faith in them. What are you standing in faith for? Perhaps for your bills to be paid, physical healing, or something else entirely. Make a list here, and take a leap of faith, believing that God will come through.

_____

_____

_____

_____

_____

_____

_____

_____

_____

_____

_____

_____

Worship Is Your Warfare

*As they began to sing and praise,
the Lord set ambushes against the men of
Ammon and Moab and Mount Seir who
were invading Judah, and they
were defeated.*

—2 Chronicles 20:22

I wish someone had told me a long time ago that worship is your warfare. This means that praise and worship activate the Kingdom of Heaven to move on your behalf like nothing else. When things weren't going my way, I used to complain, cry, and feel sorry for myself—and afterward, I always felt worse about my life and my situation. I realized that complaining hinders God's ability to move on my behalf, and I learned that praise and worship are what move God. No matter what you're facing, try praising God instead of complaining, and I promise things will begin to shift.

Think of a few things you're desiring. They could be closer intimacy with the Lord, a certain job, or a mended relationship. If things don't seem to be working out, praise God anyway. Write down a list of praises thanking God for what you're hoping He will do in your life.

Acknowledgments

Countless people, more than I can mention here, have poured into my life and pointed me on the path of faith in Jesus Christ. I thank you all.

Thank you to my family for your continual love and support: Glenn and Estella Catron, Travis Cook, Taylor Vy, and Tanner Catron—you mean the world to me!

Thank you to Awaken Church for stretching my faith. I am forever thankful for this amazing community.

Last, thank you to my Lord and Savior Jesus Christ, who saw me when no one else did and believed in me when I didn't even believe in myself. My life was forever changed when You called me to follow You.

About the Author

 **Tiffany Nicole** is the writer and founder behind the popular Christian blog Lavender Vines and the Christian greeting card business by the same name, Lavender Vines Co. Tiffany currently resides in San Diego, California, where she enjoys writing from local coffee shops and spending time with her church community. Visit the author at LavenderVines.com and on Instagram at @XoTiffanyNicole.